FRANK
Gehry

THIS IS A CARLTON BOOK

Text and design copyright © 1999 Carlton Books Limited

This edition published by Carlton Books Limited 2000
20 Mortimer Street
London
W1N 7RD
www.carltonbooks.com

A CIP catalogue for this book is available from the British Library

ISBN 1 85868 879 5

Executive Editor: Sarah Larter
Art Director: Trevor Newman
Editor: Janice Anderson
Design: Simon Mercer
Picture research: Sarah Moule
Production: Garry Lewis

Printed and bound in Dubai

FRANK
Gehry

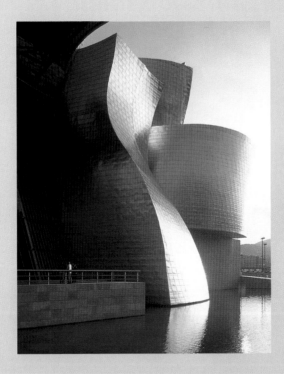

NAOMI STUNGO

There are few buildings that people will cross the

world to see. The Taj Mahal, the Pyramids, the Parthenon, maybe. Frank Gehry's Guggenheim Museum in Bilbao is one such. In the two years following its opening in 1997, more than two million visitors poured into the northern Spanish city whose principle – some would say only – attraction the museum is. Featured in countless newspapers, colour supplements and fashion magazines, Gehry's astonishing building has put Bilbao on the map – so much so that the city's airport is having to expand to keep up with demand – and has confirmed Gehry's position as the world's most famous living architect.

"The museum in Bilbao leads to a new era in building," said British architect Norman Foster at the time of the Guggenheim's opening. Gehry's friend, the sculptor Richard Serra, has claimed that "Frank represents a break with all contemporary architecture. His is not an architecture that arises from an older order. He is the first really to break with the orthodoxy of the right angle."

In reality, Gehry's Guggenheim Museum is just the most public of a long string of unorthodox buildings. Since setting up his own practice in Los Angeles in the early 1960s, Gehry's work has consistently challenged the conventions of what a building should look like. His work has ripped apart the idea of a building as a box-like container comprising four walls at right-angles to each other, a roof and a floor, replacing it instead with something altogether more fluid. The wild exuberance of the Guggenheim is simply the logical product of this process.

Gehry's buildings have created a new paradigm for architecture, one that critics Peter Arnell and Ted Bickford refer to as a "new perspective" .

What is truly striking is the public's acceptance of this idea. For some reason Gehry's architecture is not seen as "difficult" in the way much modern art is. Quite the contrary, the public flock to see his buildings, as witnessed by the popularity of the Guggenheim in Bilbao.

F R A N K

IN MUCH THE SAME WAY THAT Cubist artists AT THE BEGINNING OF THE TWENTIETH CENTURY **SHATTERED** THE single point perspective ON WHICH WESTERN ART WAS FOUNDED, GEHRY'S architecture AT THE END OF THE CENTURY PRESENTS BUILDINGS AS AN ASTONISHING **CLASH**, AN **ALL-ANGLES-AT-ONCE** EXPERIENCE.

It has taken a while, however, for Gehry to reach this position. He has now been designing strange-looking buildings for almost three-quarters of a century. Born in Toronto in 1929, he likes to describe how his grandmother encouraged his boyhood interest in architecture by helping him to make weird little structures out of scraps of wood. Part of Gehry's strength as a designer, however, comes from the fact that he is not just interested in architecture. As important an influence on his later professional development was his mother, who took the young Frank to Toronto's art galleries, helping to foster his life-long love of painting and sculpture.

Gehry was 18 when the family uprooted, leaving the familiarity of Toronto for sprawling Los Angeles. The move, Gehry later acknowledged, was an enormous upheaval that left him at once overwhelmed and fascinated by his new environment. Confused and unsure of himself,

GEHRY

Gehry eventually enrolled at the University of Southern California to study, not architecture, but fine art.

The discovery of architecture took a while. One of Gehry's classes at USC was a ceramics course taught by Glenn Lukens. Lukens took an interest in Gehry and invited him round to his house to meet Raphael Soriano, the architect whom he had commissioned to design his new place. The meeting, Gehry says, left him "lit up".

"I had just come from Canada and I didn't know anything and it was a bad time. My father had lost everything. I was really on the floor with lack of self-esteem. Not knowing what I wanted to do when I was 17 or 18 I had started working as a truck driver and I was fascinated with people who did know what to do. I was looking for a model, I guess," he recalled in discussion with Kurt Forster.

The effect of the meeting with Soriano was obvious to Lukens, who suggested to Gehry that he might enjoy studying architecture. Gehry started night classes in the architecture department. "I did really well," he says. "It was my first connection to something. They skipped me to the second year. It was a big deal." And yet, even so, Gehry had not quite found himself. He was constantly pushing at the system and testing its limits, dreaming up joint projects with the art department that, given the thoroughly traditional nature of the university, were invariably rejected.

Trying a different approach, Gehry began post-graduate studies in city planning at Harvard in 1956. He hated it and dropped out before the year ended. To fill his time, he did odd jobs and took a number of courses, including one taught by Joseph Hudnut, an architect and writer. Instead of lecturing on classical architecture in a darkened amphitheatre, Hudnut took his students on walking tours of Boston, discussing with them its "American" architecture – the city's terrace (or "row") houses, industrial buildings and other vernacular architecture.

The experience had a huge impact on Gehry. "It gave me something to strive for: creating an American architecture," he explains. "After all, I was in America, I should make American architecture. And that meant that you had to find a new language because one didn't really exist yet. It existed in the way he explained it, but the game was to find a new one."

Making your way in architecture is a slow business, though. Married by now and with a family to support, Gehry moved back to California in the late 1950s and started work as an architect, first in the office of Victor Gruen and eventually on his own. It was to be 20 years before e achieved any real fame.

In the meantime, he set about developing his contacts in the art world. Los Angeles had a vigorous artistic community. Making friends with a number of leading artists, sculptors and designers, Gehry gradually got commissions that, at last, helped him bridge the art and architecture divide. Little by little, Gehry started to develop his own very distinctively new architectural language.

His first notable project was a house and studio for graphic designer Louis Danziger and his wife Dorothy on a busy corner in Hollywood. The Danziger Studio and Residence (1964–65) took its cue both from the industrial and commercial flavour of the neighbourhood and from minimalist sculpture.

Adopting the simple cube-like form of cheap commercial buildings in the area, Gehry created two linked volumes: one for the studio, the other for the house. The drama came from the relationship between the two.

Gehry has explained "I was ... interested in the idea of connection, of putting pieces together, in a way very similar to what I am still doing 20 years later. I suppose we only have one idea in our lives."

Like the Danziger Studio and Residence, the O'Neill Hay Barn in San Juan Capistrano, California (1968), drew heavily on contemporary sculpture. The barn – part of a larger master plan for a new ranch with stables, guest house and additional buildings – was a simple structure: a huge roof and skirt of corrugated iron supported on wood posts. But by tilting the roof, Gehry gave the building a dashing abstract quality reminiscent of works by sculptors such as Carl Andre and Donald Judd.

"I HAD THIS FUNNY NOTION,"

GEHRY SAID "THAT YOU COULD MAKE

architecture

THAT YOU WOULD BUMP INTO

BEFORE YOU REALIZED IT WAS

ARCHITECTURE."

It was after seeing the Hay Barn that the painter Ron Davis asked Gehry to design him a house in Malibu (1972). The commission proved an important one for Gehry, enabling him to achieve what he had so long striven for – to establish a collaborative relationship with an artist. Lengthy discussion with Davis on perspective, geometry and illusion seemed to free up Gehry's imagination. The result was a house that broke with the conventions of the orthogonal box to a greater extent than ever before: a rhomboidal building with a steeply tilting roof which focused visitors' attention on the building's vanishing point, the nearby lake.

"I was nervous about that project," Gehry admitted long after it was built. "I thought the degree of the angles might be bizarre and make you feel uneasy. In fact, it was very restful. The building unlocked a whole lot of other possibilities for me. I spent a lot of time there, sitting and looking for a lot of days and evenings, watching the reflections. That helped me in my house. Because nothing was parallel, you couldn't predict where the shadows and sunlight and reflections would fall. If you've got a straight rectangular box with rectangular windows you sense where these things come from. But if things aren't all straight then you get a different take. That's become an interesting part of my work."

At different points throughout his career, collaborating with artists has helped Gehry to unlock ideas, to move from one stage to the next, but it would be wrong to see his work as pure art. Gehry considers himself to be first and foremost an architect. He designs buildings that function, that have gutters and drains and all the paraphernalia of real, serviceable buildings.

And yet what is so striking about his work is that he plays with the materials of architecture much as a painter or sculptor experiments with paint or clay. "There's an immediacy in paintings," he says, "you feel like the brush strokes were just made ... I wanted to see what else we can learn from paintings. In particular, how could a building be made to look like it's in process?"

"I'M AN **ARCHITECT**," GEHRY STATES, "MY intention IS TO MAKE **ARCHITECTURE**"

As his architecture gradually loosened up, Gehry increasingly accentuated the process by which he constructed his buildings, emphasizing the very timber, corrugated iron, chain-link fencing and so on from which they were constructed.

"WHEN YOU **START LOOKING** AT BUILDINGS, WHEN YOU START BEING INTERESTED IN ARCHITECTURE, YOU WALK DOWN THE STREET AND YOU SAY: 'OH LOOK AT THAT GREAT structure. ISN'T THAT GREAT? TOO BAD THEY CAN'T LEAVE IT LIKE THAT.' ... BUILDINGS THAT ARE JUST DONE BY ORDINARY PEOPLE THEY LOOK LIKE **HELL** WHEN THEY'RE FINISHED BUT WHEN THEY ARE UNDER construction THEY LOOK **GREAT**.**"**

With these ideas in mind, Gehry set about converting his own house. His remodelling of the pink, two-storey, 1920s shingle house in Santa Monica established his reputation as one of the most provocative architects of the day.

Gehry once said that he never wanted to design "pretty" buildings. "I don't look for the soft stuff, the pretty stuff. It puts me off because it seems unreal. I have this socialistic or liberal attitude about people and politics: I think of the starving kids and that do-gooder stuff I was raised on. So a pretty little salon with the beautiful colours seems like a chocolate sundae to me. It's too pretty. It's not dealing with reality. I see reality as harsher; people bite each other. My take on things comes from that point of view."

Within five years of the Santa Monica house's remodelling, 70 per cent of Gehry's neighbours had moved away. It is not hard to see why: the Gehry Residence (1978) is a seriously harsh house. Using the rough and ready materials of the building site – corrugated iron, plywood and chain-link fencing – Gehry wrapped the exterior of the house in a new skin, an awkward angular jarring layer behind which the remnants of the "pretty" original could still be seen.

"I was concerned with maintaining a 'freshness' in the house," Gehry says. "Often this freshness is lost – in over-finishing [houses], their vitality is lost. I wanted to avoid this by emphasizing the feeling that the details are still in process: that the building hasn't stopped. The very finished building has security and it's predictable. I wanted to try something different. I like playing at the edge of disaster."

Adding this unfinished-looking new layer to the outside of the house, Gehry stripped the original house back to its skeleton so that it, too, looked as if it were still in the process of being made. He took the plaster off most of the original walls, leaving just bare stud-and-lath partitions and ripped out the entire upstairs ceiling to expose the redwood roof rafters and create an enormous attic storey. Playing games with left-over pieces of the old house, he embodied them in the new design in utterly incongruous ways – an old sash window was reused as a medicine cabinet, for instance.

The neighbours may not have liked it, but the Gehry Residence marked a turning point in Gehry's career. Its benefits were slow to be felt, however. "It freaked out my developer clients," Gehry explains. "They said, 'If you like that, you don't want to deal with our stuff'." Today, he acknowledges that they were probably right. At the time, it meant that he had to start out all over again.

Gradually, however, Gehry did find clients who responded to his new-found style. By the late 1970s disenchantment with Modernism was growing and an increasing number of both architects and patrons were looking for something new. Gehry's iconoclastic style was a fresh take, a radical rethinking of what architecture could be.

To start with, commissions were, admittedly, pretty small-scale: the odd house or small housing complex, some exhibition design work. Gradually, larger

Gehry HAS NEVER BEEN AFRAID OF TRYING OUT NEW IDEAS AND STYLES. INDEED, ONE OF THE THINGS THAT CHARACTERIZES HIS WORK IS HIS WILLINGNESS TO JUNK TRIED AND TESTED IDEAS AND TO invent new ones.

projects materialized. One of the most significant was the scheme to design a new master plan for the Loyola University Law School in Los Angeles, a project that was to last, on and off, for much of next twenty years.

Gehry's buildings at Loyola (1978–) seem to mark an abrupt change from the rough-and-ready "wood butcher" look of the Gehry Residence. In part, they do. The corrugated iron and weird angles are gone, replaced by fresh stuccoed walls painted in cheerful colours.

At Loyola, a new style was appropriate: a university campus called for a less confrontational approach and, besides, the part of Los Angeles where Loyola was established was tough enough as it was without adding challenging, difficult architecture.

At another level, though, there are strong similarities between Gehry's approach at Loyola and at his own home: undercurrents that run throughout all his work, providing on-going links despite the endless changes in style.

It is easy to see why Gehry had thought he would enjoy urban design. You only have to look at his work to see his fascination with the way people move about cities and spaces, with the way buildings relate to one another. Discouraged by his experience at Harvard, he never pursued urbanism on a large scale. Instead, he has developed his ideas on a micro level – in his buildings. Very rarely, if ever, does he design a monolithic building. Instead, as he did at Loyola, Gehry tends to break projects down into a number of discrete parts, even discrete buildings, which he then links together as though they are separate buildings in a city.

In butchering his house and adding a new layer to it, Gehry created a new and unusual landscape of routes and passageways linking spaces. At Loyola he gradually developed a whole new campus, designing a string of new buildings. As important as the buildings, however, were the spaces he created between them. With its new faculties, squares and pathways, it was a city in miniature.

With the California Aerospace Museum and Theater (1982–84), Gehry again broke the building down into different parts. But here he did what he so often does: he created two completely different shaped buildings and clapped them together, bolting a metal-clad seven-sided polygon on to a pale, stone-covered rectangular building to create one dramatic volume. In much the same way that hot-dog stands in America often have a huge hot dog advertising sign, Gehry whacked a Lockheed F-104 aeroplane over the entrance, just in case there was any confusion over what the building housed.

Gehry was gradually getting bigger and bigger commissions; clients were starting to seek him out precisely because of his unusual style. Even so, he continued to design small one-off houses.

Houses seem to be a test-bed for Gehry, the place where many of his ideas get refined. The results are often pretty unusual. Take the Norton Residence in Venice, California (1982–84), a building Gehry refers to as his "pride and joy". Instead of putting the house on the (admittedly rather noisy) beachfront, Gehry placed it at the back of the long narrow lot, creating a raised observation deck for his client – who had started out as a lifeguard – at the front of the site with direct views above the traffic over the ocean.

At the Winton Guest House in Wayzata, Minnesota (1982–87), Gehry started playing with different building materials. The project, which was commissioned by a couple who lived in a 1950s Philip Johnson house, was a considered response to Johnson's sleek steel and glass pavilion.

Creating a collection of differently shaped volumes, he clad each room in a different material – Finnish plywood, galvanized metal, brick, stone, painted metal panels. It was the start of a fascination with materials that would lead, via an unbuilt house for Peter Lewis (1989–95), to the titanium cladding of the Guggenheim Museum.

By the mid-1980s, Gehry had achieved huge success – the kind of success that allows you to start doing what you want to do. With the Chiat-Day Building (1985–91), the headquarters of the West Coast advertising company, he teamed up with his friends, the artists Claes Oldenburg and Coosje van Bruggen, to create a building in which art and architecture were each as important as the other. Anyone entering the three-storey building in Venice, California, has first to negotiate Oldenburg's giant binoculars – a huge sculpture that forms the building's entrance and houses conference and research spaces.

The building was a massive logo for both Chiat/Day and Gehry. Hugely arresting, it was reproduced in countless magazines around the world. It is no surprise that, not long afterwards, Gehry won a string of foreign commissions.

Gehry has designed two complexes for the Vitra furniture company, one in Weil am Rheim in Germany, the other in Basle in Switzerland. The first, a furniture manufacturing facility and design museum (1987–89), marked an important transition: a move away from angular, geometric forms towards a much more fluid, curvaceous architecture. Always one for a pithy label, the critic Charles Jencks dubbed Gerhy's new style "vermiform". The museum, in particular, is an astonishing whirling dervish creation: an explosion of energy and shapes, of curving white walls and rakish titanium-zinc-covered roof lights that bring daylight flooding into the building's interior. Gehry developed this fluidity further at the headquarters he designed for Vitra in Basle (1988–94). Here the building is so fluid that it looks as though it was carved in ice cream that has gently melted.

By the early 1990s, Gehry's architecture was getting amazingly complicated to build. His Santa Monica studio was littered with endless cardboard models and reams of blueprints as he and his staff developed ever more complex forms and then tried to figure out how to build them.

When Gehry decided that the solution to a commission to design a retail centre for the Barcelona Olympic Village (1989–92) was to create a mall with a 49-metre (160-ft) long and 30-metre (100-ft) tall sculpture of a fish on top, the practice had really set themselves a tough design challenge. The budget was tight, the schedule tighter still. The only answer was to move to using computer-aided design software.

After extensive research, the practice eventually plumped for a French package – CATIA – developed by the aeronautics industry and used to design the Mirage fighter jet. The advantage of the program is that it allows highly complex forms to be modelled. Simply by running a laser pen, similar to those used by brain surgeons, over the surface of the cardboard models, their co-ordinates are mapped into the computer which then creates the building's skeleton and calculates the components so accurately that, even if every single piece is differently shaped, the whole thing just fits together like a jigsaw puzzle on site. It is this technology which has enabled Gehry – or rather his 120-strong staff, as he has never learned to use a computer – to design ever more astonishing forms.

Gehry is first and foremost an architect, but it would be wrong to think that his interest in creating unusual shapes extends only to buildings. Like many other architects, he has also designed furniture. Back in the late 1960s, he began experimenting with cheap materials, bending and moulding them into furniture. The result was a series of chairs, tables, chaises longues and bed frames made from cardboard. Originally selling for between $15–115, they have since become collectors' items.

ALWAYS RESTLESS, ALWAYS LOOKING AT materials

AND TRYING TO FIGURE OUT NEW WAYS OF USING THEM, GEHRY RETURNED TO

FURNITURE-MAKING IN THE LATE 1980S, THIS TIME USING

THIN STRIPS OF LAMINATED WOOD WHICH HE **WOVE** TOGETHER TO MAKE

ultra-lightweight chairs AND TABLE FRAMES. THESE

HAVE BECOME MUCH COVETED. VISITORS TO THE **Guggenheim**

Museum CAN TRY THEM OUT IN THE cafeteria.

The Guggenheim Museum in Bilbao (1991–97) is by far Gehry's best-known building. The museum has transformed the Basque capital from a post-industrial wasteland into an international tourist destination. It has proved so popular that, in its first year, ticket revenue represented 0.5 per cent of the Basque region's GDP.

When Gehry first saw the site for the museum – a run-down strip of land right in the city centre alongside the Nervion river – he realized his building needed to be both a response to the city and a dynamic new interjection into it. His competition-winning design is an astonishing building like no other: an explosion on the waterfront, a riot of tumbling shapes and forms. If it resembles anything at all, it is perhaps an enormous cargo ship or battleship. Either would be appropriate. Bilbao was traditionally the heart of the Spanish steel industry and a vigorous port. The building's titanium cladding is meant to be a sort of "memory" of this heritage as well as a beautiful polished finish that reflects what sunlight there is in Spain's wettest region.

The building has turned Gehry into an international celebrity. He is the architect that cities and organizations now want. A Frank Gehry building is considered something that adds huge cachet to a place or a brand. Over the years, institutions as conservative as banks have commissioned him – he designed the Nationale-Nederlanden Building in Prague (1992–96), as have cities reinventing themselves for the 21st century – he is currently finishing a headquarters building in Pariser Platz in Berlin (1994–2000).

Gehry continues to challenge conventions and to reinvent himself. One of the most unusual projects currently on his drawing boards is neither a headquarters for a multinational corporation nor a new cultural institution. In 1999, Gehry announced that he would design – for free – two cancer care centres in Britain in memory of his friend, the landscape architect Maggie Keswick Jencks. Keswick Jencks, the wife of the critic Charles Jencks, died of breast cancer in 1996, but not before setting up a day-care centre for other cancer sufferers at Edinburgh's Western General Hospital. The centre proved so popular that other hospitals now want similar facilities.

Design work is just starting on the Dundee centre (the other will be in Cambridge). With a shoestring budget (a tiny £300,000), the project is going to be a real challenge. Gehry is going to have to be really inventive. "We are going to have to get 'the most bangs for the buck'," he acknowledges. But then that is what he is so very good at.

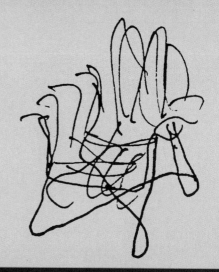
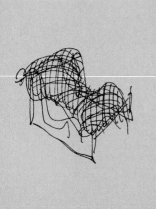
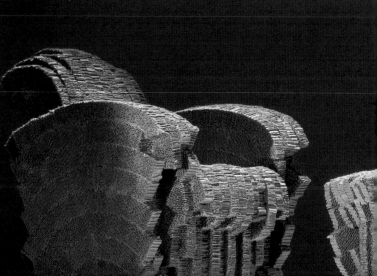

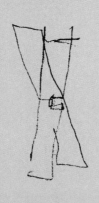
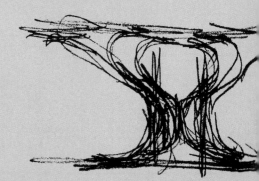

FRANK GEHRY

The architect at work in his Santa Monica studio experimenting with bent wood to make furniture.

THE LANDMARK

His design for the Guggenheim Museum in Bilbao, northern Spain, shot Gehry to international stardom.

THE INVENTOR

Whether designing buildings, like the Vitra headquarters (left), or making furniture, like this corrugated cardboard chair (right), Gehry is ceaselessly inventive.

THE FORM MAKER

The artist in Gehry is fascinated with shapes. Buildings, like the Guggenheim in Bilbao, are essentially large pieces of sculpture.

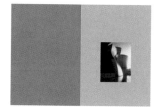

THE DRAMATIST

At the California Aerospace Museum, Gehry used billboard tactics putting a model aeroplane on the front to advertise the building's contents.

DANZIGER STUDIO AND RESIDENCE

Gehry's first important building was a house and studio (1964–65) in Hollywood for graphic designer Louis Danziger and his wife.

O'NEILL HAY BARN

The barn he designed at San Juan Capistrano in California (1968) is reminiscent of sculpture of the time.

DAVIS STUDIO AND RESIDENCE

Gehry worked closely with artist Ron Davis for this studio and house (1968–72) in Malibu, California.

GEHRY RESIDENCE

Gehry's "make-over" of his own house in Santa Monica, California (1978) was an incredible statement of intent. The house was remodelled again (1991–94)

GEHRY RESIDENCE

Gehry tore theold house apart, inserting new additions often in bizarre ways.

NORTON RESIDENCE

California, 1982–84.

SPILLER RESIDENCE

Gehry used cheap materials like wood and glass to make a series of simple light-filled rooms stacked one upon the other (1978–9).

LOYOLA UNIVERSITY LAW SCHOOL

Loyola law school in Los Angeles (1978–) marks a transition. It is more "finished"-looking than many of Gehry's buildings to date.

INDIANA AVENUE HOUSES

A series of three studio/apartments that Gehry designed for artists in Venice, California (1979–81).

INDIANA AVENUE HOUSES

Side and interior views of these studios.

CALIFORNIA AEROSPACE MUSEUM AND THEATRE

The Los Angeles-based Aerospace Museum (1982–84) was the first in a series of museum designs with which Gehry established himself.

HOUSES

Gehry used houses such as the Norton Residence (left) in California (1982–84) and the Winton Guest House, Wayzata, Minnesota, (right, 1982–87) as test cases for ideas.

WINTON GUEST HOUSE

Gehry built a series of linked rooms, each of a different shape, each clad in a different material.

CHIAT DAY BUILDING

Sculptor Claes Oldenburg worked with Gehry on this advertising agency office Venice, California (1985–91).

SCHNABEL RESIDENCE

Like Loyola Law School and the Winton Guest House, this house in Brentwood, California (1986–89) is like a city in miniature.

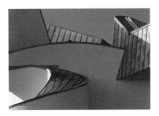

VITRA DESIGN MUSEUM

The museum at Weil-am-Rhein, Germany (1987–89 is the first of Gehry's "vermiform" or worm-like buildings, says the critic Charles Jencks. A roof detail is shown here.

VITRA DESIGN MUSEUM

There is method in the madness. The building's extraordinary exterior, left, creates a suprisingly calm interior (right), lit by shafts of daylight.

AMERICAN CENTRE

The complex forms of the American Centre in Paris (1988–94) was only possible because of the cutting-edge software in which the practice invested in the late 1980s.

VITRA INTERNATIONAL

Gehry designed a second complex for furniture maker Vitra, this time near Basle in Switzerland (1988–94).

VITRA INTERNATIONAL

Although Gehry says he is first and foremost an architect, the design mixed colour and shape just as an artist might.

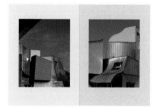

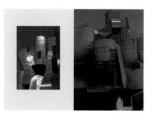

FREDERICK R WEISMAN MUSEUM

Gehry's first all-new art museum, the Weisman in Minneapolis, Minnesota (1990–93), is a foretaste of the Guggenheim. Here, the cladding is stainless steel.

GUGGENHEIM MUSEUM

Gehry's design for the Guggenheim Museum in Bilbao, Spain, won an international competition. The aim was for a landmark building that would help revitalize the city.

GUGGENHEIM MUSEUM

The titanium-clad building (1991–97) and Jeff Koons' giant dog sculpture (left) have put Bilbao on the international tourist route.

GUGGENHEIM MUSEUM

Inside, the gallery spaces are, at times, as sculptural as the exhibits.

NATIONALE-NEDERLANDEN BUILDING

This bank in Prague in the Czech Republic (1992–96) has been nicknamed "Fred and Ginger" because its two towers seem to be dancing.

FURNITURE DESIGN

Gehry has designed tables, chairs, even lamps, often from unlikely materials. His snake lamp (bottom) is made from shattered formica.

Picture credits

The publishers would like to thank the following sources for their kind permission to reproduce the pictures in this book:

Bibliography

Frank Gehry: Buildings and Projects, with an essay by Germano Celant and text by Mason Andrews. Rizzoli, 1985.

Art and Architecture in Discussion: Frank O. Gehry/Kurt W. Forster, edited by Christina Bechtler in collaboration with Kunsthaus Bregenz. Cantz, 1999.

Frank O. Gehry: the Complete Works, Francesco Dal Co and Kurt W. Forster. The Monacelli Press, 1999.